WHAT MAKES
NEWS?

WHAT MAKES NEWS?

A Three Act Play

Richard Tubb

WHAT MAKES NEWS?
A THREE ACT PLAY

This is a work of fiction. All of the characters, names, incidents, organizations, and dialogue in this novel are either the products of the author's imagination or are used fictitiously.

iUniverse books may be ordered through booksellers or by contacting:

iUniverse
1663 Liberty Drive
Bloomington, IN 47403
www.iuniverse.com
1-800-Authors (1-800-288-4677)

ISBN: 978-1-5320-8850-6 (sc)
ISBN: 978-1-5320-8851-3 (e)

Print information available on the last page.

iUniverse rev. date: 01/29/2020

What Makes News?

A three-act play set in the editorial offices of *The Global Trail*, a highly respected national newspaper.

Cast   Narrator

Ted Levi—editor-in-chief of *The Global Trail*

Susan Marples—publisher of *The Global Trail*

Liz MacCharles—investigative reporter (early fifties)

Bob Sawatski—investigative reporter (early forties)

Howard Curtis—investigative reporter (retirement age)

Jamie—newsroom gopher

Hugh Clifton—A local church small-group leader (act II)

Act I

NARRATOR, *with music over.* What makes news? Now think
about that. In today's news media, what is it that makes
news ... that people want to hear?

The night of March 14, 2019, Cyclone Idai, described
as "one of the deadliest storms on record in the
Southern Hemisphere," made landfall on the coast of
Mozambique. It brought heavy winds and rains before
moving inland to neighbouring Zimbabwe and Malawi.
By April 10, the death toll had risen to over 1,000
and due to the flooding all sources of drinking water
had been contaminated, with more than 4,000 cases of
cholera reported amongst the survivors.

How did you get to know of this *natural disaster?* Do you remember the headlines? What was your response to the news?

The very next day, on March 15, 2019, a gunman in Christchurch, New Zealand, entered a mosque when Muslims were at prayer. He killed fifty-one worshippers and injured forty-eight others. This was news and evoked a response from around the world, as it highlighted a *conflict of cultures.* Remember?

Just one month later, in Paris, a structure fire beneath the roof of the Notre Dame Cathedral destroyed the cathedral spire and most of the roof. Three emergency workers were injured in this event. The response to the news, as reported, was instantaneous. Pledges of more than a billion euros came in less than one week for the reconstruction.

You surely remember that news item! Was it *conflict, natural disaster* or something else this time?

Audiovisual communications today have enabled us to become aware of these events, without any time delay between the events and a global awareness of them—*and these events were news, with varying degrees of significance and urgency to the public.*

Some are now asking, If today's sophistication in communications had existed 2,000 years ago, would the *life, death and resurrection of Jesus Christ* have made the same impact on the news media?

It was a question on the mind of Susan Marples, publisher of *The Global Trail*, a national daily newspaper, as she sat with her editor-in-chief, Ted Levi. It was several weeks before Easter. Sitting at the conference table together, Susan explained to Ted what was on her mind. (*Music stops.*)

SUSAN, *putting down her copy of the newspaper and looking across at Ted with a concerned look.* Ted, in the history of mankind, it happened about 2,000 years ago. (*Pause.*) You know what I'm going to talk about, don't you? (*Ted nods.*) But, Ted, in its significance to you and me, it might have happened just yesterday. When it did happen, thousands of people were talking about it, and now, 2,000 years later, millions, nay, billions, are still talking about it around the world.

TED. That's true, and for many different reasons. Some believe it; some are quite indifferent to it. Some believe the event but deny the significance. Was Christ the Messiah, as He claimed?

SUSAN. That's right. So what I'm asking is this: If it had happened just yesterday, its reporting around the world could have been instantaneous and totally pervasive. Whether it would have been reported is the question I want to pose to you. What would have been the position of our paper to an event like this?

Ted, I know that you are Jewish and that this topic may be uncomfortable for you, but here's what I want you to do. Bring in three of your best investigative reporters for a discussion on this very point: How should *The Global*

Trail report an event like the death and resurrection of Christ?

Tᴇᴅ, *with a sigh.* OK. (*Reluctantly picks up the phone to talk to Liz MacCharles.*) Liz, will you come into the conference room and bring Bob Sawatski and Howard Curtis with you.

Sᴜsᴀɴ, *after appropriate greetings and when everyone is seated.* Liz and gentlemen, *The Global Trail* is an internationally respected daily newspaper, noted for its ability to investigate the significance of world events and reporting on them with integrity. As investigative reporters, you help us to achieve and maintain that reputation. (*Susan, as previously arranged, is interrupted by a knock at the door. Jamie enters.*)

Jᴀᴍɪᴇ. I apologize for interrupting, but this has just come in on the wire service, and I thought it might need your immediate attention.

Tᴇᴅ, *taking the paper from Jamie.* Thank you, Jamie. (*Jamie leaves the room. Ted looks at the wire service report, looks around, shakes his head, then reads it aloud.*)

Dateline—Jerusalem, April AD 33

Last week, a carpenter from Nazareth, who was indicted by the Jewish priests of the Sanhedrin in Jerusalem, was convicted under the Roman justice system for claiming to be king of the Jews. He was sentenced to die by crucifixion.

It is reported that this carpenter was flogged to within an inch of His life, made to carry His own instrument of death—a wooden cross—to a hill outside Jerusalem, and there was crucified by Roman soldiers. There were witnesses to the crucifixion from the carpenter's own family, including some followers who had spent the last three years accompanying Him as He spoke about the kingdom of God to vast gatherings of people and, of course, the soldiers who carried out the sentence.

After He had died—and this was confirmed by the Roman soldiers, one of whom thrust a spear into the carpenter's body, entering under His rib cage and into His heart—He was taken down, wrapped in grave clothes, and placed in a tomb. The entrance to the tomb was blocked with a huge, round stone, a seal to prevent anyone from entering, and guards were placed on duty outside to ensure that no one would have further access.

Witnesses' accounts disclose that, at the time of the carpenter's death, the curtain in the Jewish temple was torn from top to bottom, the earth shook and rocks split. Tombs of many Jewish holy people who had died broke open and the bodies raised to life.

Reports are circulating that raise a lot of questions about the man they called Jesus the

Christ, who revealed Himself to his disciples as the very Son of God.

One report states that in the morning of the third day after the carpenter's crucifixion, some ladies went to visit the tomb site, found the stone rolled away, the tomb empty and the body of Jesus gone.

Other reports are now coming in that some of His followers have actually seen the carpenter, walked with Him and talked with Him.

If these reports are true, they suggest that the most extraordinary event in the history of mankind has happened right here in Jerusalem.

SUSAN, *breaking the long silence that followed while everyone around the table looked at one another to gauge reactions.* Ted, as editor-in-chief, how are we going to report on this event in our paper? Front page or page 10?

TED, *shrugging nervously.* You know I have a bias on this issue, Susan. Maybe we should first get the response of Liz, Bob and Howard. How about you, Liz? What are your thoughts?

LIZ. Well, the report said that it was "the most extraordinary event in the history of mankind." I was asking myself how this could be the most extraordinary event in history while we are now witnessing the breakup of nations around the world and the breakdown of social order, such as we have seen daily in places like (*Slowly.*)

Bosnia ... Rwanda ... Iraq ... Afghanistan ... Egypt ... Libya ... Syria ... Hong Kong ... of course, Iran ... well, throughout the Middle East. (*Waving her arms.*) Want me to go on? Even here in North America, in the schools and on the streets of major cities. How could the death of one man possibly compare with the carnage and genocide that is going on day after day on *The Global Trail*?

HOWARD. Yes, but what if that man was indeed the Son of God, as He claimed? What if His death and resurrection was intended by God as a sign, not of a life ended but hope for a new life, a new beginning for all mankind, a new beginning in which we could all share, without all the darkness and human suffering that Liz has described? Wouldn't that place it apart and above the black and desperate events that are being played out around the world today?

BOB, *speaking matter-of-factly.* Oh, I don't know. Aren't we getting a bit buried in "religion" here? Isn't the paper really in the business of reporting what is known to be fact, without putting a religious spin on the events? Surely we should just take the wire service story, place it on page 10 and get on with the task of reporting what we can see, touch and hear.

TED, *still feeling ill at ease with the topic of the discussion.* As a Jew, while I can accept a rejection of Jesus's credibility as the promised Messiah, I cannot deny God's supreme governance over the affairs of mankind. The question that Susan is asking this morning does intrigue me. After all, we not only report on the news, but our spin on the news also helps to imprint the minds of the general public.

BOB, *resignedly*. Oh, I suppose!

TED. There are several questions on my mind. If this whole event was really orchestrated by God Himself, it would make it so much more convincing if He had "declared His shot," so to speak … if He had told His people before it happened what was going to happen. And further, how do we verify the facts of this report?

BOB. *That's* a good point, Ted!

TED. There is no doubt that this event has lived in the hearts of millions of people throughout the world for 2,000 years, which will not be the case with the events that we are pursuing with such vigour today. Will the events of today still be serious topics of everyday conversations 2,000 years from now? Liz mentioned Bosnia; are we still talking about that today? And each one who has believed in this Jewish man, Jesus, has been blessed with a peace and a hope that enables them to face this life on earth with a special and enviable joy. So perhaps the integrity of our newspaper is at stake if we do not investigate the significance of this event, in the light of world circumstances in the 21st century.

SUSAN. OK, Ted! How do we investigate these aspects of the story? Let's take your first question. Did God ever prophecy that Christ would come into this world, suffer and die and then rise from the dead? Howard, you seem to have an inkling of what it is that concerning me just now. How would you suggest we get started on this investigation?

HOWARD. This is really intriguing to me too, Ted. You see, I'm not a new Christian. I'm a baby boomer. I was born just after World War II, and my parents endured the war years, 1939 to 1945. They were firm believers and credited God with our victory over Naziism. So, I was taken to church and learned to believe in the depth of love that was extended to mankind by our Creator God. I gave my life to Christ and was baptized at eighteen when I was in college learning all about … *journalism!*

LIZ. I didn't know that, Howard. (*Casually.*) Well, you're a dark horse!

HOWARD, *with a smile.* Maybe! Well, Susan, I've been attending a small group Bible study for some time, and just last night, we were reading about the Passion of Christ in the Old Testament. I suppose it came up because Easter is in a few weeks.

TED. That's OK by me. What you call the Old Testament is found in the Torah and the Prophets, which originated with us Jews—*God's chosen people.*

HOWARD. That's right, Ted, but what we call the New Testament was also written by Jews, with the exception of a Gentile observer and follower of Jesus, Dr. Luke. In fact, the *Christian church really is Jewish!* We Gentiles are just adopted children of God, grafted, as it were, into the Jewish body of Christ.

TED. Now this gets even more intriguing for me. What *were* you reading in the Old Testament?

HOWARD. We were in the Book of Isaiah.

TED. Isaiah was written over 2,600 years ago, Howard, so, if you found a prophecy about Jesus in Isaiah, I suppose we should take note of that. Of course, you know that we don't believe that Jesus was the promised Messiah come to earth, as Christians claim Him to be.

HOWARD. I understand that. Well, we were reading in Isaiah—

TED, *picks up the phone and calls Jamie.* Jamie, would you go to the library and get the Bible that's there and bring it to us?

BOB, *standing and sounding utterly disinterested.* Hey, look ... do you need me here anymore? This is getting a little too religious for me, and I don't feel that this investigation is going to lead us to any of *today's* problems.

TED. Sit down, Bob!

SUSAN. Bob, I want you to take this seriously ... for me! (*Bob takes a deep breath and sits.*)

(Jamie enters with the Bible.)

TED. Give it to Howard, Jamie, if you will. Howard is going to find a passage there for us.

HOWARD, *looks up the passage that his Bible study group were reading.* Yes, here it is ...

See, my servant will act wisely; he will be raised and lifted up and highly exalted. Just as there were many who were appalled at him—his appearance was so disfigured beyond that of any human being and his form marred beyond human likeness—so he will sprinkle many nations, and kings will shut their mouths because of him. For what they were not told, they will see, and what they have not heard, they will understand. (Isaiah 52:13-15 NIV)

Bob. How are we supposed to know that's talking of Jesus?

Howard. Well, it may seem a stretch at this point, Bob, but it does fit the description in the New Testament of how Jesus appeared to people at the time of His crucifixion. Let me go on.

Who has believed our message and to whom has the arm of the LORD been revealed? He grew up before him like a tender shoot, and like a root out of dry ground. He had no beauty or majesty to attract us to him, nothing in his appearance that we should desire him. He was despised and rejected by mankind, a man of suffering, and familiar with pain. Like one from whom people hide their faces he was despised, and we held him in low esteem. (*Howard looks around at others to see if they are understanding the prophecy of Jesus. He continues.*)

Surely he took up our pain and bore our suffering, yet we considered him punished by

> God, stricken by him, and afflicted. But he was pierced for our transgressions, he was crushed for our iniquities; the punishment that brought us peace was on him, and by his wounds we are healed.
>
> We all, like sheep, have gone astray, each of us has turned to our own way; and the LORD has laid on him the iniquity of us all. (Isaiah 53:1-6 NIV)

LIZ. Now that's beginning to sound like the Easter story!

HOWARD. That's what I was thinking last night, Liz. (*He continues to read.*)

> He was oppressed and afflicted, yet he did not open his mouth; he was led like a lamb to the slaughter, and as a sheep before its shearers is silent, so he did not open his mouth. By oppression and judgment he was taken away.
>
> Yet who of his generation protested? For he was cut off from the land of the living; for the transgression of my people he was punished. He was assigned a grave with the wicked, and with the rich in his death, though he had done no violence, nor was any deceit in his mouth. (Isaiah 53:7-9 NIV)

LIZ. That's certainly sounding like the New Testament gospels, but why is it written in the past tense?

BOB. *That's* a good point, Liz. You're telling me that something written in the past tense is actually describing something that will happen 600 years later?

HOWARD. Time, past, present, and future are all one to God, Bob. Yes, in the New Testament, we learn that, to God, a thousand years are like a day, and a day like a thousand years. Time does not have to be specified as past, present or future—it's all one to God, but, just let me finish this piece:

> Yet it was the Lord's will to crush him and cause him to suffer, and though the Lord makes his life an offering for sin, he will see his offspring and prolong his days, and the will of the Lord will prosper in his hand.
>
> After he has suffered, he will see the light of life and be satisfied; by his knowledge my righteous servant will justify many, and he will bear their iniquities. Therefore I will give him a portion among the great, and he will divide the spoils with the strong, because he poured out his life unto death, and was numbered with the transgressors. For he bore the sin of many, and made intercession for the transgressors. (Isaiah 52:10-12 NIV)

BOB, *standing and walking the length of the table and standing behind Howard.* That's all gobbledygook to me. Surely, the Bible is just the mythological ramblings of some individual characters who lived some time in history.

TED, *addressing Bob.* That puts me in an intellectual dilemma, Bob. You see, as a Jew, I believe in the absolute historical truth of the Old Testament. But as a traditional Jew, I've been taught to reject Jesus as the promised Messiah. It's not gobbledygook to me, although I don't really want to believe what it is telling me.

LIZ, *addressing Susan.* I never was taken to church as a child, Susan, but my parents were *good* people, and they did pray to God when things got difficult for them. Before that passage was read, I prayed to God that He would give me an understanding of what He was saying. And as the passage was being read, my mind kept saying, "Wow! Really? That confirms all that I've ever learned about the Easter Passion."

HOWARD. Yes, that's how it hit me when we read it! Ted, can't you see that this does answer your question about whether God prophesied about Jesus, whom Christians call the Messiah?

SUSAN. Ted, before you answer that, maybe it's time to take a break. (*Addressing the reporters.*) Let's come back in two or three weeks, and we'll discuss this some more. Meanwhile, Howard, do you think your Bible study leader would undertake the task of leading a study just with you three investigative reporters—albeit trained skeptics?

HOWARD. I'm sure he would be delighted, and I'd be happy to set it up!

SUSAN. Please do that, Howard.

(Music up as cast leave their seats, but continue talking amongst themselves. Music softens as the narrator speaks.)

NARRATOR. Three seasoned investigative reporters, with quite different views about the history of events in a world claimed to be the creation of God, have agreed to investigate the possibility that the crucifixion and resurrection of Jesus Christ was not only factual but also the most significant event in history, heralding the fulfilment of God's plan for His earthly kingdom.

Act II

Cast Narrator
Liz
Bob
Howard
Hugh Clifton—a church small-group leader

Scene The narrator off stage. On stage, Liz, Bob, Howard and Hugh Clifton are deep in discussion about journalism: the purpose of reporting on current events and its place in preserving a historical record.

Bob is laid back in his chair, and his body language says he's not particularly convinced that this discussion is going to change his attitude towards "religion."

Liz is sitting forward in her chair, attempting as it were to catch up on what she has not been taught previously.

Howard seems to be concerned that everyone is comfortable with the assignment Susan has given the three of them.

Time A few weeks before Easter.

NARRATOR, *with soft, musical background.* This past week or so, Liz, Bob and Howard have been on their various assignments, reporting and commenting on the news in different parts of the world. Liz was on assignment in the United States, reporting on the administration's response to catastrophic world events. Bob has been following the uprising in Syria, where the forces of government there are pitted against its own citizenry and insurgents. Howard, on the home front, has been investigating domestic and street violence in urban centres throughout the nation. None are particularly anxious to get into a discussion on religion with Hugh, except perhaps Howard, who is a little protective of his church associate.

(Music stops and dialogue between them picks up.)

HUGH. So, as I understand it, you're wondering what sort of a story the Passion of Christ would be for *The Global Trail* to report on. Howard has been telling me that your publisher has been raising questions about it and asking you to investigate.

Bob, can you tell me in a word what it is that makes a good news story?

BOB, *without hesitation*. Conflict!

HUGH, *eyebrows lifted and a questioning look*. Conflict?

LIZ. Yes, it's true, Hugh. You know when you read the line "And they lived happily ever after" that you've reached the end of a story. No one really wants to read about people who are living happily together and not interfering in one another's lives. Little of what we report on in the news media ends like that. We really report on what it is that brings peoples into conflict with one another.

HUGH. I can see that. But, you know, nothing is ever *resolved* through conflict. Mostly there is a winner and a loser, or both are losers ... so, the story has no end ... it goes on, conflict after conflict.

BOB. So you see, those of us in journalism have little time for the goody-goody, warm and fuzzy things that you and your religion want to talk about. We are reporting on what is really going on in the world.

HUGH. But don't you see that what matters in the world is what God created it to be ... and what is happening in the world is not what He has planned for it to be? It brings no pleasure to a Creator God. And *make no mistake*, God has a plan to end what is happening and get the world back onto His plan for all of creation.

BOB. Of course, you're just assuming that there is a Creator God. So, if you are saying that this is His world and He is in charge, where did He go wrong?

LIZ. Hmm ... was it God, or was it people?

HUGH. Well, there is a third party that is so often simply overlooked, even by the church, when we try to account for the troubles that are visited upon the world. Let's go back a bit in history. Now, you've heard the expression "original sin," I'm sure, and you know what it refers to.

BOB. Yep! Adam crunched on an apple when God told him not to.

HUGH. Bob, you do know something about the Bible. But now I'd like to suggest to you another expression that predates original sin: I like to call it "original conflict." If I'm hearing you right, this would be your focus as news reporters. Yes?

BOB. Yep. Since I brought it up, I'll accept that premise.

HOWARD. I think I know where Hugh is going with this, but I would just like to make a point before he gets into it. You know the world seems to have accepted the *theory* of evolution as *fact,* perhaps to counter what they see as the *blind* acceptance of *creation,* and the assumption that the beginning of everything was God. So, for the purpose of our discussion, let's regard creation by a triune God as a *theory* worthy of consideration. We are not committing to it as fact, just considering it as a possible alternative to the *theory* of evolution. That is *doing our job as investigative reporters.*

BOB. Great! You're not asking *me* to accept anything on blind faith, right?

HUGH. Thanks, Howard. That puts us into "neutral" as far as our acceptance of any position we might discuss. No one should feel pressured to accept anything that I might say but rather see it as an obligation to put it to any test that you might consider necessary to move from theory to QED—"quite easily demonstrated," if anyone asks.

Well, let's go back before the beginning of time, to the very beginning of history.

LIZ. Back to Adam and Eve?

HUGH. Well, actually, Liz, we need to go back even further than that. You see, before God created Adam from the earth, He had first to create the earth.

HOWARD. Makes sense, doesn't it! I suppose we really need to go back and determine what all God actually did create ... and why. Did He have a plan?

HUGH. Good point, Howard. Let me tell you first what I believe, and I'll give you some background to my beliefs. Then I hope, at some point, you will put it all to the kinds of tests you would apply to any story that you are asked to report on. Fair enough?

(*All nod.*)

BOB, *with a shrug.* Fair enough!

HUGH. Well, I believe that there is only one Creator God, and that is the triune God of the Bible: Father, Son and Holy Spirit. And, if I renounce that belief, for me (*Indicating himself.*) that is apostasy! Furthermore, it is apostasy that puts me into a serious conflict—conflict with God Himself!

You see, for me, the Bible is *His* story, that is, God's story of His plan and purpose for the creation of everything that we can experience through our senses and intellect. The Bible is authentic *His*tory—past, present *and future.*

Bob. But surely anything that came before there were people to record events—what may have happened before Adam, if you accept that as the literal beginning of mankind— is just conjecture. How can we possibly know what happened before mankind inhabited the earth?

Hugh. Well, Bob, I don't just believe *in* God, I believe God. I believe what He says, and through His servant, the prophet Isaiah, God said, "Remember the former things, those of long ago; I am God, and there is no other, I am God and there is none like me. I make known the end from the beginning, from ancient times, (to) what is still to come" (Isaiah 46:9–10 NIV).

Here's where we have to accept the absolute supremacy of a Creator God. Surely if He can *create* mankind, He can also *inform* mankind. Not just about pre-Adamic times but about times yet to come to the world as we know it today.

How do you suppose He did that?

Bob. I have a feeling that you are going to tell us!

Hugh. Sure. We learn it today through the Word of God: the Bible.

Bob. Well, now … aren't you putting all your eggs in one basket—the Bible, a book that was written over several millennia by dozens of different authors?

H. Bob, I would like you to think of those authors as journalists, just like you. They are each writing a little bit of history, just as you are when you are reporting on events happening in the world today.

BOB. Yeah, but we are reporting on what we can see, hear or feel. That's not always the case in the Bible.

HOWARD. That's true, Bob. Moses wrote the first five books of the Bible, and he wasn't born until about 2400 or 2500 years after the creation of Adam.

HUGH. Of course, there is one major difference between you and the writers of the Bible. They know that they are writing by the inspiration of God, telling His story of creation, past, present and future. The Bible really is *His* story: of what has been, what is now and *what is to be.*

LIZ. Wow!

HUGH. Think of the Bible as a gigantic jigsaw puzzle, Liz. Each part of the puzzle is a small part of recorded history—the story of God's creation. The biblical journalists are those reporters appointed by God to tell the story, as it was, as it is *and as it will be.* As events occur and are reported upon, God's story is being revealed, and the truth of the Bible is being confirmed.

(*Holding up his Bible.*) All the pieces are in this box. There are no missing pieces. And when the picture is complete there will be no contradictions to what is written in here. When the parts of the puzzle become connected in the partially completed picture, we gradually begin to see the plan and purpose of God's creation. We begin to get the whole picture, so to speak.

BOB. Hey ... and how does that affect us as journalists today?

HUGH. Well, think of it this way: *anything* and *everything* that you report on as journalists is actually a piece of that jigsaw puzzle. Whether you realize it or not, what you report on helps to reveal God's plan for His earthly kingdom, and the picture on the box, the Bible, reveals what the ultimate disposition of that plan will look like.

LIZ. So, Hugh, what did happen before Adam and Eve came on the scene?

HUGH. Ah, now here's what the Bible tells us. In the beginning, before anything else was created, there was God— omnipotent, omnipresent and omniscient! Having absolute power to create anything He had a mind to; able to be anywhere and everywhere in His universe at once; and, having complete knowledge of every detail of His creation.

His dwelling place was heaven, and from there, He created the earth, the sun, the moon and the stars. He gave them all a name, and He had total control over them.

BOB. Man, *that* is unimaginable! At the same time, I have to admit that I cannot give an explanation of how everything came into being. I always end up saying that *they are just there.*

HUGH. I know, Bob. It's a stretch for even the keenest minds of secular intellectuals. None have been able to suggest how all that is came into being. Like you, they try to analyze what they can see, feel and hear, but without an understanding of the plan through which it all came about ... how it is progressing and what it ultimately will become ... they have no context in which they can assess the significance of their observations.

LIZ. It's beginning to make sense to me. The theory of evolution can only surmise how things that *were* evolved into what they *are*. It does not explain how they came into being in the first place.

HOWARD. I agree with you, Liz. It puzzles me why the bright minds in our educational institutions can ignore the biblical account and teach the *theory* of evolution as if it were *fact*. Please go on, Hugh.

HUGH. OK. Now, I want you to consider this: the physical universe is not all that God created before He created man. Next, He created a heavenly host of angels to help Him in His plan to have a kingdom of people, made in His image, over which He would reign as sovereign king.

BOB. Angels? You believe in angels too?

HUGH. Yes, Bob. Most assuredly. Angels are ministering spirits created to serve those who would inherit the kingdom of God.

BOB. And just who might *they* be?

HOWARD, *getting a little impatient with Bob.* You and the rest of mankind, Bob, if only we would learn to acknowledge God and learn to live in His ways!

HUGH, *reassuringly.* OK, Howard.

Angels do not have bodies of flesh and bone, but they do possess intellect and the ability to communicate. Their dwelling place is in the heavens, although they are given access to earth to serve God's purposes here.

BOB. How many of these critters do you believe there are?

HUGH. The Bible talks of "thousands upon thousands, and ten thousand times ten thousand." And certain angels were made superior in intelligence, in power and in authority over others. (*Pause.*) Know what comes next?

LIZ, *seeming impatient to get to the creation of mankind.* He made Adam and Eve!

HUGH. Sorry, Liz, but not quite. He had one more thing to do before that. He had to make a paradise dwelling place for those He would create in His image, and He chose the planet Earth for that purpose.

BOB, *with a yawn.* Hey, wait just a minute. Our publisher has asked us to investigate the significance of the Passion of Jesus Christ today! Do we really have to go back thousands of years in history to determine that?

HUGH. Look at it this way, Bob: what you are reporting on today are just a few pieces of this vast jigsaw puzzle, which gives us the whole picture of God's creation, of which we are all a part. To understand the significance of any event in history, we must put it in the context of the whole.

BOB, *resignedly.* Oh, I suppose!

HUGH. No, what came next in God's story, Liz, was the conflict that originated with the Son of the Morning, Lucifer, who was created by God with superior intelligence to be God's servant to minister to the people who would be created in God's own image to populate His earthly kingdom. But Lucifer saw an opportunity ...

BOB. Oh, yeeeaaah! This is where we come to your definition of *original conflict.*

HUGH, *encouragingly.* You *got it*, Bob! You see, Lucifer decided that his assignment to serve in God's earthly kingdom gave him an opportunity to usurp God's reign and have mankind serve *him.* Lucifer became known as Satan, which means "adversary," and was cast out of heaven. (*Finding the place in his Bible.*) Isaiah the prophet put it this way:

> How art thou fallen from heaven, O Lucifer, son of the morning! How art thou cut down to the ground, which didst weaken the nations! For thou hast said in thine heart, I will ascend into heaven, I will exalt my throne above the stars of God: I will sit also upon the mount of the congregation, in the sides of the north: I will

ascend above the heights of the clouds; I will be like the most High. (Isaiah 14:12–14 NIV)

LIZ. So then, does Satan *still* have power to influence people and bring them into conflict with one another *and* with God?

HUGH. You bet he does, Liz! The New Testament tells us that. The apostle Peter put it this way: (*From memory.*) "Be alert and of sober mind. Your enemy the devil prowls around like a roaring lion looking for someone to devour" (1 Peter 5:8 NIV).

BOB. OK … so if God is so almighty, why doesn't He deal with Satan … or with mankind, who are so misled by him?

HUGH. Think about it. You were created with a mind of your own. You can think and act on your own initiative. Would you want God to make you into a robot, not able to think for yourself, not able to decide how you want to live? Because short of destroying what He has created, that would be the only way to make everyone live as God intended from the beginning. But He created us with a free will and the ability to choose between righteousness and sin. *And sin is simply disobedience to the righteousness of God's ways.*

LIZ. Now, Hugh, you make it sound as if there is no possible answer to the conflict going on in the world. Are we all doomed to our own destruction? Does God have an answer to this dilemma? Will God give us another chance?

HUGH. Well, Liz, God has given mankind a number of opportunities to change. After He created Adam, He created Eve from Adam's rib so that together they had the gift *and the responsibility* of procreation in order to populate God's earthly kingdom. The Bible uses the term "the seed of Adam" for the means of procreation. To use a natural analogy, it is like the oak tree. One seed, an acorn, was sufficient to grow from the soil one tree with dozens of acorns, each one capable of growing a tree with dozens more acorns.

So you see, folks, Adam is an ancestor to everyone populating this earthly kingdom from the time of his creation about 6,000 years ago to now.

And know this! That *gift and responsibility* is passed down to every man and his chosen partner in marriage to this very day. Free sex and abortion were never intended to relieve man of this fundamental responsibility for procreation.

BOB. What you are saying is that there are no apes in my ancestral line? Goes against the biology I was taught in school. All my two kids are learning in school is the theory of evolution. There's no mention of Adam being a common ancestor to us all.

HUGH. Well, we agreed to take the Bible narrative as theory for the purpose of our discussion, so I will just say for now that this is what I believe, and you can determine for yourself which narrative you believe. Fair enough?

BOB. OK. That's what we agreed.

Hugh. Well, let's go on about 1,700 years from the creation of Adam. The Bible records the first expression of God's wrath, which was aroused by the wickedness of the world's population at that time. (*Finding place in Bible.*) Here's how the Bible expresses it:

> The Lord saw how great the wickedness of the human race had become on the earth, and that every inclination of the thoughts of the human heart was only evil all the time.

> The Lord regretted that he had made human beings on the earth, and his heart was deeply troubled. So the Lord said, "I will wipe from the face of the earth the human race I have created—and with them the animals, the birds and the creatures that move along the ground— for I regret that I have made them." But Noah found favor in the eyes of the Lord. (Genesis 6:5–8 NIV)

> So God said to Noah, "I am going to put an end to all people, for the earth is filled with violence because of them. I am surely going to destroy both them and the earth (Genesis 6:13).

Howard. *The Flood!*

Hugh. That's right, Howard. Noah was commissioned by God to build the Ark, which could have taken him up to a hundred years to build. When it was ready, a mating pair of every earthbound animal were then brought to Noah, and he, his family and the animals boarded the Ark, at God's command. Then came the Flood! (*Reads from the Bible.*) "The waters rose and covered the mountains to a depth of more than fifteen cubits. Every living thing that moved on land perished—birds, livestock, wild animals, all the creatures that swarm over the earth, and all mankind" (Genesis 7:20–21).

LIZ. But not Noah and his family, of course. They were saved by the Ark, which floated high above everything on earth.

HUGH. Correct! So, as Adam, through his ability to procreate, became the ancestor of everyone who ever lived, Noah, a righteous man, became the ancestor of everyone born after him, to this very day, this time through the "seed of Noah." So you see, by way of the Flood, and through Noah's offspring, God gave mankind a second chance to become a righteous kingdom.

BOB. Hey, and that didn't work, did it?

HUGH. That's a very interesting point, Bob, because it reveals something more about our Creator God. You see, God knows the beginning from the end. To Him, past, present and future are all one. So He knew that mankind would not be capable without His help to resist the wiles of the enemy, Satan. However long it might take, it was necessary to show mankind that, without acknowledging their dependence upon God the Father, they could not live righteous lives.

BOB. Are you telling me that I need God? Really? I've done pretty well so far!

HUGH. That's good, Bob, but what do you mean by "so far"? How much further in life is there to come?

BOB. Oh, I expect some time between 80 and 95, I'll depart this life, and that will be the end for me, and I don't expect anything much will happen to change the way I live in the meantime.

HUGH. How about you, Liz. Do you feel the same way as Bob?

LIZ. Oh no. I've heard something about eternal living, and I guess that it is to be either in heaven or hell.

HUGH. Well, there's some more history that we must consider. God hasn't quite given up on bringing His earthly kingdom into righteousness. Do you believe that there are Jews in the world today?

BOB. That seems like a silly question. Of course there are Jews in the world today; they're everywhere. Our boss is one of them.

HUGH. And that is a very interesting point *too*, Bob. But again, we must go back some time in history. After the Flood, God promised never again to destroy the total population in one act like a flood. That is how we got the rainbow; listen. (*Reads from the Bible.*)

> And God said, "This is the sign of the covenant I am making between me and you and every living creature with you, a covenant for all generations to come: I have set my rainbow in the clouds, and it will be the sign of the covenant

between me and the earth. Whenever I bring clouds over the earth and the rainbow appears in the clouds, I will remember my covenant between me and you and all living creatures of every kind. Never again will the waters become a flood to destroy all life. Whenever the rainbow appears in the clouds, I will see it and remember the everlasting covenant between God and all living creatures of every kind on the earth."

So God said to Noah, "This is the sign of the covenant I have established between me and all life on the earth." (Genesis 9:12–17)

Liz. So what did He try next, Hugh? How do Jews come into this story?

Hugh. What God did try next was to bring into being *one righteous nation*, to be a light to all other nations that had come into being through the nature of mankind. God chose Abram, a righteous man, to become the father of the *one nation of Israel*. Abram, now called Abraham, was father to Isaac, and Isaac father to Jacob, and everyone born thereafter through Jacob became the nation we know as Israel.

God said of His chosen ones: "I will bless those who bless you, and whoever curses you I will curse; and all peoples on earth will be blessed through you" (Genesis 12:3).

That's where we come to the Passion of Christ at last, Bob. You see, Satan was successful in setting the world in *conflict with Israel*, and there was a falling away from God's ways by His chosen ones too. As news reporters, you are well aware of what conflict has been brought into the relationships of all nations with Israel.

Clearly, humans seem unwilling to become one nation under God. Following their own self-centred ways, mankind has established their own set of rules to live by. They have dreamed up their own imperfect systems of governing, to show independence from God. They have chosen instead to live under monarchs, emperors and even dictators rather than accepting the perfect ways of our Creator. They have also invented other religious beliefs, apart from our Creator God.

Bob, do you think that this does, or at least should, *incur the wrath* of the one who created us to be His own family, "one nation under God"?

BOB. I'll hafta think about that one!

HUGH. Let me help you with that, Bob. The Bible clearly tells us that there *will be a time of God's wrath*. Speaking to Daniel, the prophet, He said, "I am going to tell you what will happen later in the time of wrath, because the vision concerns the *appointed time of the end*" (Daniel 8:19).

Yes, Bob, there is going to be a time when God will separate those who have chosen the ways of Satan, from those who have accepted the Lord Jesus Christ as their Lord and Saviour.

OK, Bob, Liz and Howard. *This is where we come to the Passion of Christ.*

LIZ. *Well, at last!* But I do see why it was necessary to go back over the history of mankind to get us to this point. I suppose I am one of those who would not want to experience God's wrath. Can't say I know much about it, but I have heard mention of a place called hell, and I don't imagine it will be any place I'd like to be.

BOB. Well, aren't you jumping to conclusions, Liz? What makes you think that hell is a place and that those who do not acknowledge Jesus Christ will be going there?

HUGH. Well, Bob, Liz and Howard, *that's precisely what the Passion of Christ was all about.* Christ was God incarnate. He came to give us the last opportunity to save ourselves from God's wrath and give Him reason to accept us into God's family, *avoiding eternity in hell!*

God knew that we were not capable of living righteous lives as long as Satan has any influence over us, and we continue to reject God and His holy ways.

As news reporters you observe and reveal to your readers all the conflict and self-promoting actions that are being played out in the world. You must wonder, *How can it end?* We could list here such things as abortion, sexual proclivity and pride parades, but of course, in those things, we would be defying "political correctness." We could also list identity theft, terrorism, rape, murder and such, and perhaps the more serious, in God's eyes, *persecution of Christians and Jews and denial of God and His righteous ways.*

BOB. OK, we don't need to list all the things that God might be angry at; we all know there is a lot wrong with how we are living in the 21st century.

HUGH. Do you remember what we read about the way God saw the world before the Flood? *The Lord saw how great the wickedness of the human race had become on the earth, and that every inclination of the thoughts of the human heart was only evil all the time.*

Do you think He might be thinking this way today?

HOWARD. Oh, *I'm* sure of it!

HUGH. Can things in the world get much worse than they are now?

As we have seen, folks, God did give mankind a number of opportunities to turn back to Him, and He has given us *one last chance—in the Passion of our Lord, Jesus Christ.*

God the Father sacrificed His own Son to take the punishment that each one of us deserves for our indifference to His righteous ways. As we have seen through the Flood, the only other option for God to rid the world of sin was to destroy everyone in it! Accepting the punishment of death *to Himself,* Christ now gives us an opportunity to avoid God's day of wrath, which will come in the end times.

If we, individually, will seek that forgiveness for our sin and acknowledge Jesus Christ as our Lord and Saviour, we will be accepted to live eternally in the family of God.

No more monarchs, emperors or dictators—just one Lord and Master in Jesus Christ. No more isms: communism, socialism, capitalism, Naziism, liberalism and conservatism, to name just a few. We become one body of believers: the body and bride of Christ, the Church. We will serve *and be served by* our Lord Jesus.

HOWARD. Bob and Liz, you will remember me saying that I accepted that offer of forgiveness when I was just eighteen. I accepted Christ into my heart and was baptized shortly after hearing a message like this when I was in college.

HUGH. Thank you, Howard. No regrets?

HOWARD. Nary a one. I've made a few mistakes along the way, but I have always felt secure in that forgiveness.

HUGH. So you see, Bob and Liz, one day, sometime in the future—we don't know the day and the year—you will either be undergoing God's wrath, or you will be observing that event from a place in the clouds. Christ will harvest His bride to be with Him, in the event that has become known as the Rapture.

And that is what we will be celebrating and thanking God for at Easter.

Easter, as we have come to know it, is very much like the Passover, where those who identified themselves as God's own in Egypt were spared the plagues that were set upon their slave masters, the Egyptians.

HOWARD. I suppose we now have to consider how we, as investigative reporters, will report back to our publisher. Can we continue to separate our reporting of current events from the bigger picture of world history *as we find it in the Holy Bible?*

LIZ. Hmm! I wonder what Susan Marples will be expecting us to report?

HOWARD. I suggest we try to be honest and reflect our true feelings and thoughts about this assignment, even if it means we'll be swimming against the tide of modern journalism—and maybe looking for jobs!

BOB. Looking for jobs, Howard? How do you figure that?

HOWARD. Well, if the current education system refuses to allow any study of the Bible in schools, and if the theory of evolution is taught as fact, how can a public influenced by popular educational practices possibly accept our newspaper expressing a counterview: biblical history?

Do you think our publisher will risk the possibility of losing the paper's readership?

(*Turning gratefully to Hugh.*) Thank you, Hugh. You're a good storyteller—*His* story, that is!

(All continue talking with one another, with soft, musical background.)

NARRATOR. Bob, Liz and Howard have been given a brief but thorough run-through of Bible history, leading up to the Passion of Christ, which will be celebrated shortly in many different ways. To some, the statutory holiday gives them a break from their daily work routine. To others, it will be an opportunity for family or friends to come together over a long weekend. For others, it will be a time of reflection and church attendance, celebrating the death and resurrection of the Lord Jesus Christ.

To the three investigative reporters, they must now decide how they will each communicate back to the publisher of *The Global Trail* whether it is an event in world history that should influence their reporting of current events ... or not. *That, ultimately, will be a decision for the publisher, Susan Marples.*

Act III

Cast Ted Levi
        Susan
        Liz
        Bob
        Howard

Time A week or so before Easter.

Scene The editorial office of *The Global Trail*. awaiting the entry of Susan Marples and Ted Levi. Howard, Liz and Bob are awaiting the entry of Susan Marples and Ted Levi. They still seem to be uncertain about how they should present their findings with the publisher and are engaged in some rather hurried discussion. For the past couple of weeks, Liz, Bob and Howard have been discussing just how they could present their opinions as one report to the publisher, Susan. They were unable to agree.

Susan and Ted enter the room and exchange greetings with the three reporters, who stand respectfully.

Susan, *indicating for them to sit down.* Good morning, Liz, Bob and Howard.

Well, it's been three weeks now since we met here to discuss an assignment of mine. Meanwhile, you have been on assignments for Ted. I've been wondering: Has my assignment had any influence on you in the way you have tackled Ted's? (*With a shrug and a questioning look.*) Have you written up your articles any differently than you would have done before?

BOB. Well, I wasn't quite sure that that was what you wanted us to consider. It was certainly interesting to hear what Howard's church associate had to say about *his* beliefs, but that's what they were—*his beliefs*—and I could see no reason to report things that we are assigned to cover any differently than before.

We are in what is called a post-Christian era now, and that's OK by me! Sure, there's a lot of conflict going on in the world, and it is something that we have to face and find answers to. But we know that it takes time to get everyone thinking along the same lines, and if we report things as we see them so that those in authority—or government—can identify appropriate responses, that's about all we, as news reporters, can be expected to do. Tell it like it is!

SUSAN. What will you be doing this Easter, Bob?

BOB. Well, if Ted does not have me on assignment somewhere, I will probably be on the golf course for a large part of Friday, Saturday and Sunday, relaxing down there in Hawaii.

SUSAN. Thank you, Bob. The Passion of Christ is old history and is not much to celebrate in the 21st century. Is that correct?

BOB, *with a shrug.* Pretty well.

SUSAN. How about you, Ted? Easter weekend is special on the Jewish calendar too, isn't it?

TED. Well, yes, but not to celebrate the Passion of Christ. That's when we celebrate the Passover. And that is also in the Bible, describing how God gave Jews an opportunity to avoid His wrath, which was to be poured out on Egyptians for their enslavement of His chosen people.

SUSAN. Yes, Ted. I know that story well. That's when God parted the Red Sea so that the Israelites could walk over in safety and not be caught by Egypt's army. (*Ted nods.*)

Let's ask Liz now how she feels about the assignment I gave them. Liz, do you feel the same way as Bob?

LIZ. Not exactly. I've still much to learn about world history from a biblical perspective, but I do see how Hugh's reasoning makes the theory of evolution seem foolish. I just cannot imagine that there may be a pair of copulating apes in my ancestral line, however far back that could have been. No, I can certainly see how we can all count Adam and his helper, Eve, as our original ancestors.

SUSAN. No argument there, Ted?

TED. Not from me!

LIZ. Then, if that is true, the rest of history as recorded, or revealed, in the Bible becomes plausible. And I will hafta get reading it a little more often. Check—I'll hafta *start* readin' it!

HOWARD. Not a bad idea, Liz.

LIZ, *with a smile and a glance at Howard.* Looking at all the conflict in the world today, I can see how a Creator God could get awful mad at people for messing up His vision of how He wanted people to live.

But you asked us, "Have you written up your articles any differently than you would have done before?" There are two concerns I have with that question. One is this: Do I have any right to put my spin on events, taking that responsibility away from the reader? For that reason, I just see it as my responsibility to report on events exactly as they happen, being as accurate and truthful as I can be.

SUSAN. Good point, Liz.

LIZ. The second concern is with what we all identify now as political correctness. Although we have the presumption of free speech in our country, any reporting on my part that would indicate a position on topics like abortion, gay marriage, Islamism or even evolution would get me and our paper into semilegal problems. I can just imagine crowds of protesters outside our doors, demanding women's rights, homosexual rights, freedom *of* religion, freedom *from* religion in our schools, and on and on. As publisher, Susan, would you be prepared to take on the responsibility of incurring the ire of angry crowds, demanding that you not downplay the assumed rights of minority groups whose conduct does not exactly fit a biblical standard?

SUSAN. Hmmm. (*Pause.*) Howard, we haven't heard from you. What are your thoughts on the assignment I gave you?

HOWARD. Frankly, I'm seriously challenged.

TED. Challenged, Howard? I've never known you to complain about any assignments I've given you, and your write-ups have always reflected the integrity of *The Global Trail.* How has this assignment of Susan presented a new challenge to you? You're not thinking of retiring are you?

HOWARD. Well, I could retire, I suppose, and claim a good pension. But I'm thinking seriously of my responsibilities as a child of God. Should I think of it in the context of my responsibilities as a news reporter?

TED. I've always appreciated your work, Howard.

HOWARD. Thank you, Ted. Over the years I've been a Christian, I have tried to live my life in accordance with my beliefs. There have been some highlights and a few failures, but on the whole, I have considered myself to be living the good life. Now, as I have taken seriously the assignment that you gave us, Susan, I recognize that I have been riding the tide and not really thinking seriously about why Christ had to die such a painful death to take the punishment that was deserved by *everyone*—not just non-believers or anti-Christians. As the Bible says, "We have *all sinned* and fallen short of the glory of God."

So, is it enough that I can rest on my laurels, telling myself, hey, there are enough professionals in the pulpits of our nation. Why does God need me to be some kind of witness to a wicked world? Or does God ask something more of *me* as a believer?

BOB. I guess you're wanting to turn our paper into a mouthpiece for God, hey, Howard?

HOWARD. OK, Bob. We know your feelings towards this assignment. But look, I believe that it is God's command to "love the Lord our God with all our heart, soul, and strength, and love our neighbour as ourselves." What about all those non-believers, like you, and anti-Christians in the world? As they cross my path, in one way or another, aren't they all my neighbours?

Aren't those who read my news reports my neighbours? If I really believe that Christ took upon Himself the punishment we deserve, saving us from God's wrath, should I be avoiding talking about this plan God had for our salvation when He committed His Son, Jesus Christ, to take such punishment?

SUSAN. Go on, Howard. How do you find this a challenge?

HOWARD. When God tells us clearly in the Scriptures that a time is coming when His wrath will be poured out on those who live in disobedience to Him, should we not recognize that inevitability in our recording of world history? We have an audience, and we have the communication skills to convey the "truth." Not every pastor has those communication skills, and let's face it: they don't have the audience that we do. It is most likely that almost all pulpit sermons are delivered to the already converted. Non-believers and anti-Christians don't walk through the doors of our churches—except, perhaps, for terrorist purposes.

SUSAN. I sense that you are you passing the baton back to me, Howard. Do you think the paper should set a policy of accepting the Bible's record of history, past, present and future, as the basic thread connecting all the events about which we report?

HOWARD. I suppose I am, Susan. In a way, your assignment to us now brings that challenge back to you. If you accept the Passion of our Lord Jesus Christ as authentic and that the Bible is itself authentic world history, past, present and future, are you prepared to allow *The Global Trail* to be one of God's witnesses to a wicked world, showing the way to salvation to our neighbours?

(Lights dim, and soft music over the narrators closing comments.)

Narrator. The coffee room and desks in *The Global Trail* offices will be abuzz with discussions on this topic that has been raised by its publisher, Susan Marples. Don't end your subscription but watch to see what the future will be for *The Global Trail*. Will it set a new trend in news reporting, referencing the Bible's narrative outlining world history? Or will the status quo prevail?

Printed in the United States
By Bookmasters